Aloneness is a

Many-Headed Bird

by

Rosie Jackson & Dawn Gorman

"to focus on one moment of joy..."

for darling Annie

much love always

Rosie

October 2020 xxx

First published 2020 by The Hedgehog Poetry Press,

5 Coppack House, Churchill Avenue, Clevedon. BS21 6QW

www.hedgehogpress.co.uk

ISBN: 978-1-913499-45-7

Contents

The dialogue begins with 'Treadmill' by Rosie Jackson then continues alternately.

Treadmill

I love darkness, the weight of it, the way
it presses on me like a lover. But it's the light

I love most, lying awake in summer waiting
for that gentle bleaching of dawn, when the wheels

of the day start to turn, dreams blur on the horizon,
and birdsong seems to bring back friends newly gone.

I hear them beseech me to do the living for them,
to not forget what being in a body is, what love is,

what the body is capable of when it loves.
And doubtless I will miss it too: the closeness of skin

on skin, mouth on mouth, those cries that sound
like someone else. Can anything lift the soul

into rapture the way love-making can?
Not that sex should be the measure of anything,

but in our world it often is. I confess I too do
what women my age do: whittle years off my age

with running, lipstick, yoga, slide into size 8 jeans.
But the treadmill is moving faster than I can run,

each day a scramble up the chute that tips us towards landfill.
How can we age gracefully in a culture that makes death the enemy?

Truth is a Wild Thing

When I am gone, you will find me here,
where swallows swoop over dandelion clocks
in the meadow, and small winged things
dip and bob above the water in the trough.
What will I miss? The sun's warmth
on my face, the tickle of cow parsley against
bare arms. But will I still love the vetch's
melody of purples? Will I still love at all?
Perhaps, released from senses, I will simply
be all of this – the fuzz of a bumblebee,
that rook's caw, the fragrance of this day.
I come here now to take a break from writing,
and to stock up with – what is it?
A kind of truth I'm hungry for these days.
I know the way of things – that if I were
this chestnut tree, I would not offer pyramids
of flowers, but, already autumned,
would be heavy with conkers, waiting
for the first to fall.
But with age comes empathy,
and I am as gentle with the woodlouse
ravelled in pet hair on my kitchen floor
as with the no-chance man who turns up
for the date, all hope, new jeans and *Eau Sauvage*.
My mother used to say of women my age
'She's let herself go', but while I keep
myself in shape, I think there is a letting go
available, a different kind of love,
if we are wild enough to take it.

What Is It Makes a Man?

When I meet a man these days, I no longer ask
the old ritual question 'And what do you do?'

but 'Who are you?' – I want to know what kind of vessel
he's become, how he lives in a body that must be lost.

Not that I'll ever know long-term coupling now,
like one of those 1940's film scenes of a pair in a train carriage

as vistas of exotic landscapes are pulled across the window
behind them. I have spent too many years being driven

into sidings. That last marriage especially – strong man,
house in the country, redemption song – how quickly it went wrong:

bullying, covert abuse, the whole thing a grand illusion
that took longer to get over than the time it lasted.

We fought over the silliest things. I remember he used to refuse
to remove his huge watch in bed, said he felt naked without it.

I said it symbolised his attachment to power. I thought about that
today, when I read about Sworn Virgins of Albania – women

who've renounced sex, stepped out of their gender,
so they can live as men do: inherit property, smoke,

wear watches. Sex probably is worth renouncing
for some things, but to be able to tell the time?

All that Glitters

Laura from my class at school
has had three facelifts –
can't bear the thought that men
will no longer find her attractive.
She was having the second
while my friend, my rock, Amanda
was in surgery for breast cancer,
didn't make it.
Strange, the things we think are essential.
Carol from work is 64 and still on HRT –
says she knows she should come off it
but has always been a sexual being,
it's her identity, doesn't want to lose it.
I get that, notice the tell-tale glitter
the hormones dust her with –
the kind I used to see mid-month
in the mirror. I remember, too,
the trouble those fertile windows
ushered in, the alleycats.
I tried HRT but felt I was betraying
my body's own good sense
(Get out girl, while you can).
God knows, she and I have had enough,
all those bloody men,
too much screaming, too much booze,
too many lies (mostly theirs),
the idiot who said
he kept his eyes closed during sex
so he wouldn't fall in love.
The thing about hormonal retreat
is it shows me who I really am –
someone who doesn't shout, but listens,
hears the groan of the wheel of the world,
steps up, presses her shoulder to it.

Untouched

I am ashamed of buying into the shame of my body
as it ages. It makes me think of my mother,

widowed in her early fifties, who spent
the next forty years untouched. By anyone.

A few days before she died, I helped wash her.
What I didn't know was that her womb

had fallen completely outside her body. No one knew.
Even a doctor had not come close enough.

It explained her refusal to ever take a bath,
why she was ashamed of herself as a woman,

a stranger in her own old body, why she shrank
into self-loathing and fear. But we all live in bodies

that are going to betray us. If we could think of death
as something more winsome, perhaps we could learn

to love these vehicles we're trapped inside, festoon them
the way Indians bedeck their beaten-up trucks

each year with ribbons, garlands of jasmine,
marigold, grateful to be carried safely thus far.

Bloodlines

Weak with flu, I climb my family tree.
Members of the DNA website
have been there before me,
lift me high into branches
where grandparents reach back
through time to their own young selves,
love multiplying as it divides
away from me.
My lips find for the first time
names my blood remembers –
Samuel Nightingale, Agnes Blythe,
Silence Blackham, Joseph Swain –
the feverish mantra of my own making.
All that coupling.
Chances are, my Esthers and Janes
had no time for doe-eyed dreams,
took their best chance for security, escape.
But I hope some of them ached for their man,
and later, when it was their bodies that ached,
he leaned in to rub their shoulders.
What would they make of me,
walking from so many men?
Envy my freedom? Pity me?
I love my solitude, would rather wake
to the natter of sparrows under
centuries' old eaves than to some man's
flicked-on radio beside me, early news.
But the visit of an old lover
brought something home –
to wake in the dark of night
to the sound of another, breathing,
took me back to where we began –
not the smallness of us, but to
animal skins, the howl of wolves,
the ancient contract of how to survive.

The Ground We Stand On

My grandfathers were blackened by seams of coal.
Tibshelf, Sutton, Pleasley, Clay Cross, Glapwell,

were my family's scrag end of the woods, slagheaps
our mountains near the landlocked spine of the country.

The green bit on the map was Hardwick Hall,
where my mother knew Bess' family tree better than her own.

Mum left school at fourteen to work in a stocking factory where
her mother, Emma, a widow, had lost three fingers in a machine.

My father, by day a rat catcher and meat inspector,
by night a poet, recited Shakespeare at supper (we called it tea),

much to my mother's displeasure. She longed for a real bloke
who could mend cars, win the pools, have a backbone

that wouldn't cave in to illness as Dad's did. All the virtues
I loved him for - kind, generous, God-fearing, tender -

were too mild for my mother, who wanted a Rhett Butler -
and she put my father down till he lay, far too young, in the earth.

Torn between the two of them, I was caught between loving men
and despising them; the dilemma compounded when I drowned

in the second wave of feminism. It takes a long time
to find our life's work - to learn what real loving is.

It All Adds Up

I come to this poem from the 1901 Census
in Clay Cross, where huge families
in four-roomed miners' cottages were tallied
like cattle at the bottom of the page:
'Total of males and of females'.
Working stock, breeding stock.

In the '60s, Mum took me there on the bus.
The air stank of coal when we got off,
and Nanna's house whispered of things
I'd not known – tin bath in front of the fire,
my coal hewer grandfather,
beer on his breath, what happened next.

One time, a little girl turned up,
took me to see her kittens.
Her house was jammed with children
fighting over a cardboard box
and I, no siblings, shy and six
ran back to Nanna's in tears.

At my house there was order, order,
my birdwatcher Dad obsessively
ticking off species on lists: printed cards
for how many, what, where.
He tried to get me interested but I hated it –
blackbirds didn't need a name to sing.

These days, I see that wish for me to join him
was his way of trying to warm the coldness
between us, and feel a rush of regret,
late love for an old man trapped
in a crumbling body,
counting down.

Floored

I try to erase the day my father died, because pulling it
out of history's python mouth brings shame sticky as coal dust.

I was a student, we had no phone, emergency calls came
through a neighbour in the flat below.

My mother told me the news (I'd not known Dad was ill),
and I was trembling as I lowered the heavy black mouthpiece,

shivering so much my neighbour held me close
in what I thought was sympathy, then laid me on the floor –

it was uncarpeted – and fucked the shock of the news
and the shock of the sex into me so it never left

and I can never think of my father's death
without feeling unclean. I feel sick as I write this down.

I've never put it into words before. My son was a toddler.
I went back up to our attic flat, to his unsteady steps, still shaking,

I couldn't stop shaking. My husband thought death
was the reason, but it wasn't. My son is now almost the age

my dad was when he died. Yet those varnished floorboards
are as hard and knotted as they ever were. How does that man,

I wonder, recall that afternoon? With pride? Remorse?
Has he brought up his daughters to be feminists?

Can I forgive him? More importantly, can I forgive myself
for not giving my father a better ending?

Running

What if I could reach her, my student self,
touch her arm in Eastbank Street,
say *'Don't go'* when the nightclub DJ
asks her back to his bedsit by the railway.
Chances are, she'd be too drunk to listen.
She doesn't know him, tells no one.
It's what, 3am? There's a sofa, coffee table,
bed to the left, kitchen units to the right,
the only door straight ahead, key still in the lock.
Him making tea. What makes her count
the number of strides it would take to get out?
Does he spoon in the sugar too slowly?
He puts down the drinks, sits beside her,
and there he is, moving in, the usual stuff,
nothing more – then suddenly
he leaps like a lynx on top of her,
pins her down, crushes her flat,
his voice in her ear (the matter-of-fact tone)
'I want to squeeze all the air out of you.'
At which she is fish, slippery, slides out,
is over the table, stride, stride, stride,
key, stairs, gone, long legs running,
heart, mouth, pavement, no looking back.
Maybe he tries to follow,
maybe just sits with his tea (did she spill it?).
But sometimes, in the night, I do look back,
and it's not like lights seen from a train –
it's there on the track, train coming.
I run, keep running.

The Light We Can't See

My friend Linda, a poet, died unexpectedly this week.
She was ten years younger than me. I keep seeing her

that afternoon at one of my classes, when a mallard
had wandered onto my back lawn (God knows why).

Linda was the one who knew how to approach it, talk to it, coax it
into a box and take it home to her pond. She was practical like that.

The shock of mortality changes things, makes them clearer,
scissors black silhouettes against sunlight like a daguerreotype.

For years, I wanted to be like a man, to put my feet under
their privileged table. Now I'm happy to not belong,

to spend my time wresting mercy from its opposite,
beauty from mud and grit. I don't care any more who wears

the medals or feathers, I'm just thankful to have arrived
at the harvest of myself, to have come through, able to look back

on all the wounding as someone trying to stab water. And when I think
of Linda, I can't help catching some exuberance,

as if death is the same kind of excitement that comes each morning
when darkness lifts. That simple happiness.

Anamnesis

When my daughter was two years old,
she told me she was once my mother.
Her face was urgent, the little frown
an un-forgetting between her eyes.
She said she could still hear us
'behind the wall',
that I was the middle
of her three daughters.
I looked at the solid silence
of that ordinary bedroom
and felt microscopic
in the presence of the giant
that had entered, unseen.
There is so much I do not know.
But what I have learned
is that there are worse things
than death.
There is forgetting.
And there is forgetting to love.
The ones who remember
stare into the face of the dark,
and shine.
Keishaye Steede forgave
her 17-year-old son's killers.
That beautiful boy.
That extraordinary gift.

The Hanged Man

The morning after Linda's unexpected death, her partner
walked out onto their land and in his agony cried out to her,

'*Where are you? Linda, where* are *you?*' And as he uttered
the words, hundreds and hundreds of starlings rose

from the thicket nearby, till the sky was dark with them.
He doesn't believe in anything supernatural. To him,

even metaphor is an indulgence. But he knew the birds
must be some kind of message. I admit there are times

I wish I too had no sense of anything beyond this world,
wish I were blinkered totally, able to concentrate only

on what's in front of me: days when the world capsizes
and I remember too much, as if we are nothing but shadows

of ideas, and when the curtain lifts, the light wanting to enter
is too much to see. I don't speak of it much, even in poetry.

In the past, such notions took you to the stake – Bruno, for one,
who felt, as I do, that God is immanent, everywhere,

was hung upside down, naked, burnt in the market place.
It's easy to make a mockery of mystery.

I've learned not to put my secret knowings into words,
but hold them close in the darkness, like the sun at midnight.

Hard News

** Some names and identifying details have been
changed to protect the privacy of individuals' (Newspaper etiquette)*

After Roger's* funeral, the old team gathers
at some pub near the crem for dried-up
cucumber sandwiches, mushroom quiche,
and the chance to gauge each other's success.
Sarah*, who now holds the fort, tells me
I'm a luvvie now because I write poems
not 'hard news', and I just smile because
we both know it took two years for her to twig
that I spent lunchtimes in bed with the editor.
News. I still remember the glee in Rachael's*
eyes, how she clapped her hands, said *'Good story'*
when a fatal came in, car crash, local lad.
The words stuck somewhere
between my stomach and lips. *Heartless bitch.*
But listen, it was press day, we still needed
a front page lead and she was doing her job.
Twenty years on, fresh deaths flutter
in racks outside petrol stations.
But to fuel the other in us, when people
were mown down for their faith in Christchurch,
the town's mayor Lianne Dalziel told reporters:
*'The only way that communities can respond
to the voice of hate is to come together in love,
compassion and kindness.'* What would Roger say,
who loved to work in his garden, plant out
seedlings, watch things grow? What would
they all say, once the story is over?

Yet

Just when I'd given up, in the midst of friends dying
and hormones falling away, I've met someone –

a man, a little younger – and I'm almost believing love
is once more possible. I've long wanted this, waited for this,

prayed to fall in love one last time. And how delicious it is
to lift away that island feeling. He makes me laugh,

that's what I like most, his lightness of being. I'd forgotten
how spending time with someone you like dismantles the heaviness,

and though fears rise like mosquitoes from wetlands,
I'm determined to take each hour in its own wonder.

Yesterday, I was teaching all day: women aged sixty to ninety,
writing their life stories, harrowing the way for what girls, now,

mostly take for granted. Hilarious tales of convent schools
and sex education: being told never to sit on a boy's lap,

but if you do, be sure to put down a thick sheet of newspaper first.
'No,' piped one woman, *'in our school it wasn't newspaper*

we had to put down. It was a telephone directory.' We needed
the laughter after stories of divorce, lost fathers, poverty.

To focus on one moment of joy, one memory of flying, skating,
to become a ninety-year old unable to pick up her stick for cackling,

though her husband is long gone, her teeth gone, her faith in God
gone – yet how happy she is to be bent double with raucous laughter.

Aloneness is a Many-Headed Bird

My landlord, the one who wrote a novel
called *The Journal of a Coffin Dodger*
and encouraged me to write,
peered into my newborn son's cot
and said *'You'll never be alone now'.*
He knew there was no man to speak of
but I was never sure if he meant this
as a blessing or a curse.
Living on Benefit, my world was small.
But it's in the spaces that life really happens,
and what I see now is there's contentment
in the humdrum: silver domes of rain
on someone's brolly in the queue for the bus,
the quiet of the flat once my baby was asleep,
and it was hands and knees on the floor,
cutting pattern pieces from old
sixth-form summer dresses
to make miniature shirts and dungarees.
Lifting up a sleeve, or pocket,
I would see the shape of what was gone.
Happiness is something we chase
like butterflies in a meadow,
even when it's right there, in our net.
I think of this today as I sit in a field, alone,
and watch the broad wings of buzzards
smooth out the creases from the sky.
Walkers gabble past, seem to see nothing,
not even me, and I wish for them
a space into which some light,
or the thrush's song, might fall.

How Can We Bear It?

When we are ready, people are sent to help us surrender
to the not-knowing. I was sent George Barker, T.S. Eliot's protégé,

who knocked on my office door one afternoon,
introduced me to a poet's invisible oceans and cities.

I'd invited him to read to a group of undergraduates,
but only a handful turned up. What did they care

about an ageing, priapic poet, incantatory and fearless,
who had fathered fifteen children?

It wasn't for them he came, his words hypnotic, passionate,
singing of Blake and Yeats. It was to awaken me,

to make me see the concrete wasteland of a modern campus
through his eyes: the 1960's architecture, windowless corridors,

left-brain questions on the wall. As soon as he came
through the door, he gestured around us, looked me

in the eye and asked, '*How can you bear it?*' That seed of a question
would lever me out of my prestigious job, and I snaked down

the ladder that was leading to a professorial chair and stout pension.
From then on I was no longer a shoulder-padded academic marching

to the city with a brief case, but a poet in a short red dress,
garlanded by poppies, heading west in search of her tribe.

Folly, of course, from a worldly point of view, to fall
under the spell of words, to live so near the breadline.

But it taught me to hear things in shells, to notice the in-between,
the weeds *(les mauvaises herbes)*, the hidden path, interstices.

Midnight with the Conservationists

On a beach in Cape Verde,
a newly-hatched loggerhead turtle
small as a spoon on my palm
swims the air with flippers.
The moon calls it to the water.
Its mother, long-gone when it hatched,
said nothing about predators, fish hooks.
Didn't mention to her daughters
it would be nearly 30 years
before they came back to this beach
to lay their own eggs,
nor that only one in a thousand
would live that long.
I tell my children what I can.
We stoop together to release
our turtles on the sand.
Years later, they will tell me truths
they think they have just invented.
For now, I hold this moment –
small lives beginning a journey,
and two moons:
one, a beacon,
the other a glitter of fragments
scattered on the sea.

Better than Angels

That murmuration of starlings I saw at new year
on the Somerset levels: four million of them, giant ink blots

in the sky melding into dark formations above water and peat.
I posted photos on Facebook: #better than angels.

The universe, thank God, is more intelligent than we are.
The soul in everything: *animus mundi.*

If it takes another flood to bring us to our senses,
it will happen. Everything is connected.

Even as being in a body gets harder, we have to let our selves
be worn away, dissolve, till we are more river than rock,

able to move with the current, tide, pull of the moon, to become
as transparent as spirit, compassion sitting inside us like water.

Vickie McCray, the woman from Tennessee who contracted
AIDS from her bisexual husband, then nursed him till his death,

nursed her sister too, contaminated by the same man.
Vickie forgave them both. Love without hair splitting.

Love that puts itself in the balance, light as a feather,
yet muscled enough to carry the world.

Hands Like Ours

Last week I was in Sheffield, back to my roots.
My bones remembered the sound of the ground.
Outside the cathedral a small gathering
drew us in, my old lover and I –
there was no panic of something bad,
no accident, musician, ranter, clown,
just rich calm, quiet watching,
a communal breath, held.
What was this magical thing
that transfixed so many people?
(And let us not speak of gender, religion, race –
let us choose just to be people).
It was a fully-grown brown rat.
Some reason, perhaps age or illness
had caused the animal, that small,
complete being of itself,
to patter slowly, quietly over paving slabs
in broad daylight, searching the gaps,
enjoying the sunshine, washing its ears
(with 'hands' not so different from ours).
A young person crouched close by
to film it on a phone. Another sat with two
children on steps a stride away,
all giggles at their own braveness,
but clearly in love with the moment.
That potent symbol of invasiveness,
danger, death, gazed at in our intolerant times
with benevolence – even the man at my side
smiled, touched my hand.
We are capable of more love than we know.
That's something to reach for, isn't it,
in the dark of the night?

Rosie Jackson

Author Photograph © G. McKerrow

ROSIE JACKSON was brought up in Yorkshire and the Midlands and now lives in Devon. Her poems are widely published. *What the Ground Holds* (Poetry Salzburg, 2014) was followed by *The Light Box* (Cultured Llama, 2016) and her memoir *The Glass Mother* (Unthank, 2016). Rosie has taught at the University of East Anglia, UWE, and Cortijo Romero, Spain. Poetry awards include 1st prizes at Poetry Space 2019, Wells 2018, Cookham 2017. *Two Girls and a Beehive: Poems about the Art and Lives of Stanley Spencer and Hilda Carline Spencer* (written with Graham Burchell), was published by Two Rivers Press, 2020.

www.rosiejackson.org.uk

Dawn Gorman

Author Photograph © A.S. Nash

DAWN GORMAN is a freelance editor, radio presenter and poetry writing tutor & mentor. She devises and runs community arts events, including the monthly reading series Words & Ears in Bradford on Avon, and works closely with other writers, artists, photographers, musicians and film-makers: her collaborative film poems have been shown at festivals on four continents, including Cannes Short Film Festival. Her pamphlet, *Instead, Let Us Say* (Dempsey & Windle, 2019) won the Brian Dempsey Memorial Prize, while *This Meeting of Tracks* (Toadlily Press, 2013), was published in the Pushcart Prize-nominated four-poet book *Mend & Hone*.

www.dawngorman.co.uk